Sweet Legacy

Carol
I've always loved
having you for my
sister and my friend
Love Barb

a Sweet Legacy

TRADITIONAL CANDY

MAKING MADE EASY!

Many Blessings from
my kitchen to yours!
Shelley Rippy

SHELLEY RIPPY

TATE PUBLISHING
AND ENTERPRISES, LLC

Published by Tate Publishing & Enterprises, LLC
127 E. Trade Center Terrace | Mustang, Oklahoma 73064 USA
1.888.361.9473 | www.tatepublishing.com

Tate Publishing is committed to excellence in the publishing industry. The company reflects the philosophy established by the founders, based on Psalm 68:11,
"The Lord gave the word and great was the company of those who published it."

Published in the United States of America

ISBN: 978-1-61346-930-9
1. Cooking: Methods, Baking, Candy Making
2. Family & Relationships: Activities, Cooking
12.02.14

Dedication

This book is dedicated to my grandmother, Mary Rumbaugh, who has always believed that no matter how many advancements this world makes, there are a few "old fashioned" things that every young person should know. Even though she was a full-time registered nurse and mother of three, she always took time to plant and tend a garden, pickle and can the vegetables, and create magnificent jams and jellies for the family to share. She has established a long tradition of crafting handmade gifts from her sewing room and her kitchen. She has given away beautiful quilts and soft snuggly baby blankets. She took the time to help me sew my Halloween costumes when I was young and my bride's maid dresses when I got older.

She spent the last five years of her nursing career as a Hospice nurse, traveling all over southwest Missouri and northern Arkansas. She helped her patients complete their quilts and took them fresh jam and candies that we would make over a long weekend every autumn.

Everywhere she went, she enriched someone's life with her handmade creations. She has managed to pass her drive and determination and just a few of her many talents on to her daughters and grand-daughters. Now that is a *Sweet Legacy*!

They will still bear fruit in old age, they will stay fresh and green…

Psalms 92:14 (NIV)

Acknowledgements

I have been collecting favorite candy recipes for many years, often jotting down little notes or fond memories on the back of the recipe to read and enjoy later. It was my mother, Sue, who first pointed out to me that I was collecting the "bones" of a real cookbook. She encouraged me to write *A Sweet Legacy* to share these family favorites and preserve them for my children and theirs.

During the time that I was collecting these family recipes and writing this book, my mom and I discussed the concept of leaving a legacy for our children. My mom reminded me that leaving a legacy is less about material things you leave your children and far more about what you do with them throughout your life. I want my own legacy to my children to include fond memories of family and cherished weekends of candy making.

I have thought about this concept a lot. I want my legacy to convey the message that candy is the "result," but it is the process of candy making that really matters. For me, the process of making candy is special. It involves the people that I love. What is truly important in my life is the time that I spend with my family. That is why I call this book *A Sweet Legacy*. The relationships I build with my children, my family, and my friends while making candy is the sweet legacy that I leave to them. A legacy is not always money. That is an inheritance. Leaving the legacy of love for your children first requires relationship with them!

I want to thank my family, especially my mother, Sue Wilson; my grandmother, Mary Rumbaugh; and my aunts, Linda Madden and Paula Wolcott who took the time to dig through old index cards to locate half remembered and often faded copies of the recipes we all had enjoyed since our childhoods and that we knew were "just lying around here somewhere!"

They patiently helped me test and retest these recipes to make sure that each would turn out exactly as described here.

Finally, I want to thank my editors, without whom this book could not exist.

Candy Making Supply List

People have been turning out wonderful candies for generations, so it's clear that most candies do not require a lot of "special equipment." But we modern cooks do like our gadgets, and there are a few items that may make the difference between good candy and wow-that's-the-best-I've-ever-tasted candy.

There are two reasons that candy recipes fail. One is failure to properly measure the ingredients. The other is not using a candy thermometer. Now, my grandmother can consistently make caramel without a thermometer. Me? I can make a batch of brown sticky goo or something resembling an old-fashioned slow sucker if I don't use my thermometer! If I want a consistent product every time, a candy thermometer is a *must*. Using the right equipment and watching the temperature closely will help you produce consistent texture and taste each and every time you make your favorite recipe.

- **Candy thermometer – The kind in a glass tube has always worked best in our kitchens.**
- **Set of dry measuring cups**
- **Set of standard measuring spoons**
- **1 cup, 2 cup, and 4 cup liquid measuring cups**
- **Cornstarch**
- **Cooling racks**
- **Dipping spoons – These are available at Michael's or Hobby Lobby.**

- Candy molds (For chocolates with lemon cream)
- Cookie sheets
- Wax paper
- Foil candy wrappers (available at craft stores or online and great for fudge)
- Wax coated candy wrappers (available at stores or online and great for caramel or taffy)
- Storage containers, such as Ziploc containers or tins
- Saran Wrap – Original please!
- Large, heavy saucepan – 8-quart size is great for double recipes of caramel
- 10-inch or 12-inch iron skillet
- Electric stand mixer, 5 or 6 quart capacity
- 9x13-inch glass baking dishes
- Loaf pan
- Wooden spoons and spatulas
- Silicone spatulas
- Small foil or holiday print paper mini candy cups
- For gift giving: baskets, cellophane, and ribbon

Table of Contents

Candy-Making Supply List 9

Preface 13

Introduction 15

Prologue 17

Almond Roca 19

Almond Toffee 23

Brazil Nut Chews 27

Buckeyes 31

Candy Bar Filling 35

Caramel Corn 39

Caramel Nut Rolls with Divinity Centers 43

Chocolate-Coated Coconut Balls 47

Chocolate-Covered Cordial Cherries 51

Cream Caramel 55

Creamy Date Candy 59

Fudge	63
Chocolate Walnut Fudge	67
Glazed Almonds	71
Crunchy Glazed Walnuts	73
Honey Almond Nougat	77
Mexican Orange Candy	81
Molded Chocolates with Tart Lemon Filling	85
Peanut Clusters	89
Pecan Toffee	91
Buttery Pecan Pralines	95
Chewy Pecan Pralines	99
Popcorn Balls	103
Molasses Popcorn Balls	107
Pulled Molasses Taffy	111
Old-Fashioned Vinegar Taffy	115
Rum Truffles	119
Turtles	123
Afterword	127
Tips and Tricks	129
Terminology	133
Cooking Measurement Equivalent	137
Endnotes	139

Preface

Like most modern families, the women in my family lead very busy lives. Careers, husbands, children, and the activities that go with them make it difficult to carve out time for traditions or reunions. However, we have managed to save a handful of annual traditions. One, especially, has become a very important event for our family and even for our grateful friends. We all come together one long weekend each fall for what has become a candy-making marathon.

We have preserved this "sweet legacy" by passing it down to generations of our children and sharing it with "in-laws" who marry into our family. This candy-making weekend binds us together as a family, generation to generation, and ensures the bonds of friendship within the family remain strong.

Candy making is a bit of a dying art. Large chains and automation have made it relatively inexpensive and, perhaps unnecessary, for the average cook to know what it means to "spin a thread" or cook to the "soft ball stage." Beautiful gourmet candy is readily available, especially around all of the "Hallmark Holidays." So one has to wonder, *Why am I writing a cookbook about candy making?* The answer: because candy making *is* a dying art and candy making is only partly about the candy!

There is nothing as personal as receiving a handmade gift. Imagine a brilliant jar of handmade, individually wrapped caramel pieces or a box of beautifully packaged rum truffles. Nothing says, "You're special!" quite like a handmade confection.

a Sweet Legacy

Anyone can be a successful candy maker. When you look at a beautiful truffle with its silky, smooth coating, it is easy to believe that it's magic. But by following these simple directions, you can easily create equally beautiful confections to rival any on the market today.

This small collection of old-fashioned candy recipes truly is *A Sweet Legacy* from our family to yours.

Introduction

Candy making has been a tradition in our family for almost one hundred years.

My great-grandmother, Jessee Louella Place, was born in 1899. After high school in 1916, she went to work in a confectionary in Iola, Kansas. She soon learned how to make fancy dipped chocolates, candies, and other confections.

After WWI, she moved to Amarillo, Texas, where she met Joseph Tipton Tate. In 1921, she married Joseph Tate, and the couple went on to have four daughters and one son.

The recipes she had learned at the candy factory, she adapted and taught to her children.

When she was in her sixties, she worked as a cook at the School of the Ozarks* (now called the College of the Ozarks) near Branson, Missouri. At that time, the annual family candy-making enterprise would produce approximately one hundred pounds of homemade confections each year. She would take her share of the candy to work where she would distribute it to all of the tables for the students and staff to enjoy during the holiday season.

My great-grandmother made candy with her daughters and granddaughters until the end of her days. These are her recipes.

*The School of the Ozarks provided educational opportunities for underprivileged children.

a Sweet Legacy

Prologue

A typical candy-making weekend in our family happens only once a year, around the holidays. On that special weekend, we go through about eighty pounds of sugar and twenty-five pounds of butter.

17

a Sweet Legacy

Almond Roca

My relationship with my aunts has blossomed in the kitchen, and we have become great friends. It's amazing what you can learn about each other over a boiling pot or a large pile of candy needing to be wrapped. At first, I would find myself calling one of them to boast of a recipe done right or to get advice on how to package a particular gift. It wasn't long before I was seeking their advice on more important subjects, like home and family.

a Sweet Legacy

Almond Roca

2 c. butter or margarine

2 c. sugar

6 T. water

2 T. light corn syrup

1 c. coarsely chopped almonds

8 oz. or 3/4 c. milk chocolate chopped (I prefer semi-sweet chocolate chips)

1 c. finely chopped almonds

Melt butter in a heavy 2-quart saucepan; add sugar. Stir over medium heat till sugar dissolves. Add 6 tablespoons of water and the corn syrup.

Cook over medium heat, stirring often, to soft crack stage (290° F), for about 12 minutes. (Watch carefully after 280° F.) Remove from heat and quickly stir in coarse nuts.

Spread on buttered baking sheet.

Wait until the candy stops trying to spread; then sprinkle the chocolate chips evenly over the top. They will quickly soften to a spreadable consistency. Spread the melting chocolate over the toffee using the back of a spoon or a silicone spatula.

Sprinkle with finely chopped nuts.

Allow to cool on counter top or chill to firm. Break in pieces. Makes 1 and 1/4 pounds.

a Sweet Legacy

Almond Toffee

This recipe is shockingly simple to make. Yet everyone will be so impressed with the results!

The chocolate is optional for this recipe. I like to make some with and some without so everyone is happy! But if you have small children in the house, watch out! You may find little fingerprints in the chocolate topping. It is so hard to wait for it to completely cool before sampling a bite!

a Sweet Legacy

Almond Toffee

3/4 c butter

2/3 c sugar

1/3 c light corn syrup

1 c whole raw almonds

2 3-oz. chocolate chips

In a 10-inch skillet, melt butter over medium heat. Stir in remaining ingredients except chocolate chips. Continue cooking, stirring constantly until almonds pop and mixture is a golden brown in color (15-20 minutes). I like to hear at least 3 "pops" from the almonds before I call it done. Pour onto greased 9-x-13-inch cookie sheet, and spread candy to fill most of that area. Sprinkle chocolate chips over candy. Spread melting chocolate over toffee, using the back of a spoon or a rubber spatula. Cool completely and break into pieces. Store toffee in an airtight container in a cool place.

a Sweet Legacy

Brazil Nut Chews

Winter is a great time for candy making. When you run out of room in the fridges and freezers, you can use "natural cooling" in the garage to store the candy until it can be packaged. I often wonder what my great-grandmother would think if she could look into my grandmother's garage and see every countertop and every car hood, trunk, and top completely covered in containers of candies in various stages of completion.

a Sweet Legacy

Brazil Nut Chews

1 c. granulated sugar

1 c. brown sugar

3/4 c. water

1/2 t. salt

1 t. butter

4 c. chopped Brazil nuts

1 c. dark corn syrup

1 lb. dipping chocolate, optional

Combine sugars, water, corn syrup, and salt. Stir over low heat until dissolved. Cook to 245º F. The candy will form a slightly firm ball when dropped in a bowl of cold water. Remove from heat. Add butter and nuts. Pour into buttered 8-x-8-inch pan. Allow candy to set and cut into 1-inch squares. Dip in chocolate. Or drop by rounded teaspoon onto greased pan or slab. Allow to cool and wrap in wax paper.

a Sweet Legacy

Buckeyes

Note from Aunt Paula, December 10, 2005:

Dear Shelley,

It suddenly occurred to me this morning that our cooking weekend last year was only a few days before Dad died. I found myself several times last weekend being close to tears and couldn't understand why. I really miss Dad. He used to love our family gatherings and loved to be the "official" taster in the kitchen. For some reason, I feel his loss more this year than last…

My grandpa always looked forward to our candy-making gatherings, probably as much as we did. He loved having family and friends around, and there was no shortage of "samples" for him to try.

a Sweet Legacy

Buckeyes

1 lb. butter

2 lb. peanut butter

2 1/2 lb. powdered sugar

Mix by hand (the dough should be pretty stiff, but not too stiff) and form into balls the size of small walnuts. You may need to refrigerate the dough so it won't be too sticky. Place on a cookie sheet or tray, and freeze overnight.

Chocolate Dip for Buckeyes

12 oz. semi-sweet chocolate chips

12 oz. milk chocolate chips

1/2 slab of cooking wax

Melt in a double boiler and dip balls, leaving the tip of the peanut butter dough exposed. This will make them look like a buckeye nut. I usually stick a toothpick in them to hold on to while I dip them in the chocolate. Eat the ones that fall off the toothpick. Place on wax paper to dry. Store buckeyes in an airtight container in refrigerator or freezer.

Hint: When dipping dough, have balls frozen so they won't fall off the toothpick into the chocolate. It makes dipping easier and forces you to eat fewer mistakes… Makes about 100 balls.

a Sweet Legacy

Candy Bar Filling

Once my children started school, I realized that candy makes a great teacher's gift. Teachers love getting consumables. After all, how many statues of apples can one person have? Every fall, my sister-in-law, Sarah, and I discuss how many teachers each of our children want to gift and plan time to make and package the candy together. We enjoy finding little boxes and tins to really show off the lovely candy inside.

Candy Bar Filling

1 c. sugar

1 c. brown sugar

1 c. light corn syrup

1 c. water

1/4 c. dry egg white and 3 T. water

4 T. melted semi-sweet chocolate (optional)

1 t. vanilla

1 lb. dipping chocolate

In large saucepan (6 quarts) combine sugar, brown sugar, corn syrup, and water. Bring to a boil over medium heat with lid on. (Watch carefully or syrup may boil over.) Once candy comes to a full boil, remove lid and continue cooking to 238º F or just to the soft ball stage. Stirring is not necessary.

Before syrup reaches 238º F, start egg whites/water beating. I start mine once syrup reaches 225º F. This gives plenty of time to beat the egg whites and doesn't leave them sitting too long. Beat until stiff.

When candy reaches 238º F, continue beating egg whites, and slowly pour syrup into beating egg whites. Continue beating until mixture is thick and fluffy. Fold in melted semi sweet chocolate and vanilla.

Pour into buttered 9-x-13-inch dish and allow candy to set. I prefer to chill the candy before cutting with a sharp, buttered knife. Cut into 1-inch squares and dip in melted chocolate. This candy filling is very similar to the filling in Milky Way and Mars bars.

a Sweet Legacy

Caramel Corn

All kids love caramel corn. It's just a fact of life! And caramel corn is surprisingly easy to make. You can add crunchy, glazed walnuts or glazed almonds for a yummy variation. Toasted pecans are also delicious. But my own kids prefer their caramel corn without the nuts.

My neighbor, Rhanna, makes the best caramel corn every fall. If we are heading out of town for the holidays, she always gives us a tub of her caramel corn before we pull out of the driveway. We snack on that caramel corn all the way to Texas. I hope she isn't expecting us to share it with our relatives in Texas… All we arrive with is the empty bucket!

a Sweet Legacy

Caramel Corn

6 qts. popped corn

2 sticks butter (1/2 pound)

2 c. dark brown sugar

1/2 c. dark corn syrup

1/2 t. baking soda

1/2 t. vanilla

SHELLEY RIPPY

Butter a large bowl or baking pan. Fill with popcorn. In a medium saucepan, bring butter, brown sugar, and syrup to a boil over medium heat. Boil for 5 minutes. Remove from heat. Add baking soda and vanilla. Stir well, and pour over popped corn. Mix well using a large buttered spoon or spatula. Pour caramel corn into a large buttered pan and bake in oven at 250° F for 1 hour. Stir every 15 minutes while in oven to prevent sticking and burning.

Cool and serve!

You can add raw, candied, or toasted nuts to this recipe before placing in the oven for a yummy variety. Try adding the crunchy glazed walnuts for a delicious treat.

a Sweet Legacy

Caramel Nut Rolls with Divinity Centers

It doesn't matter how old we get, we all start calling for Grandma as the SME (Subject Matter Expert) to hurry to the kitchen whenever the caramel nears the soft ball stage.

I realized this year that the SME for caramel nut rolls is actually me! When did I achieve the status to claim that title?

Note: If you are making the caramel nut rolls, it will take 3 recipes of the caramel to one batch of the divinity. It is important to make the 3 recipes of caramel separately, though, because the rolls must be prepared while the caramel is hot. I make this caramel in a 10-inch or 12-inch cast-iron skillet. A double recipe will boil over when the evaporated milk is added. So it is best to make a single recipe.

This is a delicious caramel with a very different texture and flavor from cream caramel. If you don't feel like making divinity, this caramel is excellent just with nuts. It is our favorite caramel for turtles!

a Sweet Legacy

Caramel Nut Rolls with Divinity Centers…Truly Divine!

Divinity for Nut Rolls

1c. sugar

1/2 c. light corn syrup

1/2 c. water

2 egg whites, beaten until stiff peaks form.

SHELLEY RIPPY

In 8-quart saucepan, combine sugar, corn syrup, and water over medium high heat. Boil, without stirring, until it spins a long thread. Continue cooking until candy makes a firm moldable ball when dropped in a bowl of cold water. Remove from heat, and beat with an electric mixer or by hand until mixture is white and foamy.

While candy is cooking, beat the egg whites. Add egg whites to candy, one spoon at a time, and beat until creamy. Discard the last 2 spoonfuls of egg white. Pour into warm greased and floured 8-x-8-inch pan to cool. Cut cooled divinity into strips, approximately 1 inch wide by 3 inches long. Divinity should hold its shape and be manageable. However, if your divinity is too soft, don't panic. You can roll short strips in cornstarch to keep them from sticking together or to the wax paper. Chill or freeze. Divinity needs to be cold so it doesn't melt into the hot caramel. Roll chilled divinity strips in warm caramel, and then immediately roll in the chopped nuts. Place completed log on wax paper and chill or set in cool place to keep it from losing its shape.

Divinity can be made ahead and stored in freezer for up to a month or a refrigerator for 1 to 2 days before use.

Dipping the divinity into the caramel works best with two people: one person to dredge the divinity through the caramel and into the nuts, the other to roll the logs and move the completed nut roll out of the way.

Pecan or walnut, why choose? I like to do some of each and wrap them in different Holiday print cellophane papers. I find it is best to keep them short, 3 to 4 inches. They will grow as you coat and roll them. Also, a small log is not so daunting to the person who wants to indulge and eat the whole thing!

Two pounds (approximately) of finely chopped pecans or walnuts are needed for caramel nut rolls. We have had great success using the grating blade of the food processor to finely chop nuts.

Spread nuts in a thick layer in a jellyroll pan or on a large platter. It's a good idea to put a sheet of wax paper under the nuts to keep the hot caramel from sticking to the platter.

a Sweet Legacy

Caramel for Nut Rolls

1 c. sugar

1/2 c. light corn syrup

1 12-oz. can evaporated milk

1 stick butter (1/4 lb.)

5 Large Marshmallows

Brown sugar in large iron skillet or heavy stainless skillet, stirring constantly with a wooden spatula to keep sugar from burning. Sugar will become chunky and then melt into liquid and turn golden brown. Remove from heat and add evaporated milk, stirring constantly. Don't panic. It *will* foam up and a mass of solids will form. Keep stirring with a wooden spatula even though it looks hopeless! Caramel will become smooth very quickly. Add butter and syrup, and cook to soft ball stage. Set off heat and beat with a wooden spatula. Add 5 large marshmallows to help caramel set. Beat until smooth.

When thick, dip cold divinity sticks and roll in nuts. If it gets too thick while you are rolling the divinity, you can reheat the caramel over boiling water. If you run out of divinity, just drop spoonfuls of remaining caramel into the nuts for a yummy variation.

Once nut rolls are completely cool, cut pieces of Saran Wrap and wrap each roll. We recommend then rolling candy bars in clear holiday-pattern cellophane and tying the ends with colorful ribbons. They look like little party favors.

If you are making the caramel nut rolls, it will take 3 recipes of the caramel to one batch of the divinity. It is important to make the 3 recipes of caramel separately, though, because it must be put together while the caramel is hot.

Chocolate-Coated Coconut Balls

Coconut is a funny thing. Most people either claim to love it or hate it. But coconut has been used in candy making for generations, and coconut confections are often remembered as a childhood favorite.

This recipe came from a friend of my grandmother's many years ago. She got it from a cookbook compiled by telephone operators when she worked for the telephone company in 1921. This old candy may soon be your new favorite!

a Sweet Legacy

Chocolate-Coated Coconut Balls

Coconut Filling

2 boxes (1 lb. each) powdered sugar

1 large package coconut

1 12-oz. can evaporated milk

1 stick butter (1/4 lb.)

1 to 4 c. chopped pecans (medium fine), depending on preference

Coating

16 – 24 oz. semi-sweet chocolate chips

1 stick paraffin

Mix butter, milk, coconut, nuts, and powdered sugar with hands and roll into small balls about the size of a small walnut. Place coconut balls about 1 inch apart on a cookie sheet or jellyroll pan that has been lined with wax paper or nonstick foil. Chill until firm (freezing makes easier to dip). Melt paraffin in double boiler. Add chocolate chips and stir to melt. Stick toothpick in chilled balls and dip in chocolate. Shake off excess. (Dipping spoons/forks may also be used.) Place on waxed paper. Let set until chocolate is firm. Store in airtight container. Makes about 100 balls.

a Sweet Legacy

Chocolate-Covered Cordial Cherries

My Grandma just seemed to "know" how to cook. When I was small, I'd follow her around the kitchen begging to help. She would tell me to add a "dab" of this, a "smidgen" of that, or a "tad" of the other… She was always throwing out sayings like "a pint is a pound the world around!"

When I decided this book needed to be written, I really had to work to change her "tads" and "dabs" into measurements the modern cook could comprehend!

When you say fondant, most people probably think of the decorations on a really fancy cake, like a wedding cake. It's also used for little French petit fours. But most people don't realize that fondant is actually the most commonly used center for chocolate butter cream candies, lemon candies, and even chocolate-covered cherries. Fondant is a very versatile ingredient for many chocolates because it is smooth and creamy and takes well to having flavors added.

51

a Sweet Legacy

Chocolate-Covered Cordial Cherries

Chocolate-covered cordial cherries must be stored in the refrigerator for 1 to 2 weeks before serving to allow the candy to ripen and centers to liquefy.

60 Maraschino cherries (2 jars)

1/2 c. Amaretto liquor

3 T. soft butter (soft, but not melted)

3 T. light corn syrup

2 c. confectioners' sugar

1 lb. dipping chocolate

Medium mixing bowl

Small saucepan

Cookie sheet

Paper towels

Wax paper

Plastic storage container

Drain the cherries over a bowl. Reserve 1/4 cup of the cherry juice. Bring it to a boil in a small sauce-pan. Remove from heat, and stir in 1/2 cup amaretto. Stir in the cherries. Cover and let stand in refrigerator overnight.

Remove the cherries and place them onto a plate lined with paper towels. Allow them to sit for 1 to 2 hours, or until well drained. You may wish to transfer them to a fresh paper towel lined plate after an hour to allow further draining.

To make the fondant, place the butter in a medium-sized mixing bowl. Add corn syrup and mix well. Stir in confectioners' sugar, and knead it until it is smooth. You can use your hands to do this. If the mixture is too soft, place it in the refrigerator to chill until you are able to knead it like dough.

Divide the fondant in half, and leave one half covered by plastic wrap to prevent drying. Form the half you are working with into a ball. Slightly flatten into a thick disk, and using a table knife, cut the dough like

a Sweet Legacy

a pie into 8 equal portions. Each segment can be cut into 4 equal pieces to wrap 4 cherries. Each piece of fondant is just over 1/2 teaspoon.

Line a large cookie sheet with wax paper. Shape 1/2 teaspoon to 3/4 teaspoon of the dough around each of the maraschino cherries by flattening it between the heels of your hands and forming a circle. Gently flatten the fondant until it is large enough to wrap the cherry and press back together around the stem. Place the covered cherries upright on the cookie sheet. Repeat this process with the other half of the fondant.

Chill coated cherries in the refrigerator until firm, about 1 to 2 hours.

Melt the dipping chocolate according to package directions. I always do only half of the bag at one time to avoid having to reheat the chocolate and risk overheating. Hold each cherry by the stem and dip into the chocolate. Use a spoon to coat completely. Make sure each cherry is completely sealed with chocolate, or the cherry juice will leak out.

Allow the excess chocolate to drip off of the cherries before placing them, stem side up, on a cookie sheet lined with wax paper. Chill the cherry cordials for 2 to 3 hours, or until the chocolate has set. Cherries may weep around the stem. Any openings can be sealed with a bit of dipping chocolate.

Place the candies into an airtight plastic storage container in the refrigerator. Leave the container in the refrigerator for 1 to 2 weeks to allow the centers to soften and liquefy.

Cream Caramel

Our relationships have bloomed in the kitchen over a pot of boiling caramel or across the table as we laugh about how the number of pecan logs has multiplied in the refrigerator overnight. We have no recollection of making so many!

Just as the simple ingredients of sugar, syrup, and cream come together to make these delightful confections, our family bond becomes richer through the time and effort we spend producing, wrapping, and gifting these confections to family and friends.

When it is time to wrap the caramels, we have 4 generations participating.

a Sweet Legacy

Cream Caramel

(I always double this recipe)

2 c. sugar

3/4 c. light corn syrup

1/2 c. butter

2 c. half-n-half cream, divided into 1 c. portions

SHELLEY RIPPY

Butter an 8-x-8-x-2-inch pan for a single recipe, or 9-x-13-inch pan for a double recipe. Combine sugar, corn syrup, butter, and 1 cup of half-n-half in an 8-quart heavy saucepan. Bring to a boil over medium heat, stirring constantly. Stir in remaining 1 cup cream, and cook to boiling, stirring constantly.

Reduce heat and allow to boil, stirring occasionally, until candy thermometer reads 245º F (firm ball stage).

Immediately spread mixture evenly in the well-buttered pan. Allow to cool. Cut into 1-inch squares, and wrap in original Saran Wrap or waxed twisting paper wrappers. Each recipe makes 5 dozen.

*This recipe can be made with or without nuts. I find that the candy will stay smoother and creamier longer without nuts. But if you plan to eat it soon, pecans are a great addition!

a Sweet Legacy

Creamy Date Candy

Gathering to make candy the first autumn following my Grandfather's death was bittersweet. He used to sample all of our creations and comment, "This is kind of musty... Musty have another!"

And you could always count on Grandpa to eat our mistakes.

This is a fabulous recipe for date candy. It is unusual and simple to make with a texture similar to creamy fudge. The "old timers" called this date loaf. It's delicious with nuts, but it stores longer without nuts.

Creamy Date Candy

2 c. heavy cream

2 c. sugar

8 oz. chopped dates

1 tsp vanilla

(optional – 1 c. chopped nuts)

Cook cream and sugar to 230° F while stirring constantly. Slowly add chopped dates while maintaining boil. Continue stirring and cook to 237° F. Remove from heat, and continue stirring until boil stops. Add vanilla and beat by hand until candy begins to thicken. Pour into buttered loaf pan and cool completely.

Slice cooled candy into wafers about 1/4 to 1/2 inch thick, and wrap in foil wrappers.

Watch temperature carefully. Consistency should be chewy like cream caramel. Overcooking will cause candy to be fudgier.

a Sweet Legacy

Fudge

Candy just brings out the best in people, and everyone has their particular favorite! When we invited our dear friend, Kathy, to come make candy for a weekend, her response was immediate:

Shelley,

Can we make fudge? Mmmm. Fudge…how can I resist. I would love to come.   As long as there is fudge, I'm there!

a Sweet Legacy

Fudge

4 1/2 c. granulated sugar

2 5-oz. cans evaporated milk

3 12-oz. packages semi-sweet chocolate chips

2 c. nuts (My aunt Paula's copy of this recipe says, "No nuts, please!")

1 pint jar of marshmallow cream

1/4 lb. butter

2 t. vanilla

Butter a 9-x-13-inch pan and set aside.

Put chocolate chips, nuts (if using), marshmallow cream, butter, and vanilla in a large mixing bowl and set aside.

Bring sugar and evaporated milk to a boil in a medium saucepan over medium heat. Reduce heat to low, and continue to boil for 7 minutes, stirring frequently to prevent burning. Pour over remaining ingredients and stir until melted.

Pour into buttered 9-x-13-inch pan. Chill. Cut into 1-inch squares and store in airtight container (I prefer tins).

This is our favorite fudge recipe because it is "no fail" fudge!

a Sweet Legacy

Chocolate Walnut Fudge

The great thing about fudge is that there are so many varieties. Five different people may say fudge is their very favorite candy but may describe five totally different flavors! The one constant, though, is the creamy texture of a good fudge. It is a delicious combination of sugar, butter, milk, and other flavors like chocolate, peanut butter, white chocolate, butterscotch, or walnuts. So many choices!

a Sweet Legacy

Chocolate Walnut Fudge

2 c. granulated sugar

1 5-oz. can evaporated milk

12 oz. semisweet chocolate chips

1 c. coarsely chopped walnuts

10 large marshmallows

1/2 c. butter

1 t. vanilla extract

SHELLEY RIPPY

TRADITIONAL CANDY MAKING MADE EASY!

Butter an 8-x-8-inch glass dish. Put butter, chocolate chips, and vanilla in a mixing bowl and set aside. Combine sugar, milk, and marshmallows in a medium saucepan over medium heat. Bring to a boil, stirring frequently. Reduce heat to low, and continue cooking 6 minutes more, stirring constantly. Remove from heat. Pour marshmallow mixture over contents of mixing bowl. Using a wooden spoon or strong plastic spoon, beat entire mixture until it thickens and loses its gloss. Quickly fold in nuts and pour into prepared pan. Refrigerate several hours until firm.

a Sweet Legacy

Glazed Almonds

This simple candied-almond recipe is one of the first I learned to make "all by myself"! It is simple, and children are delighted with how quickly and easily the recipe comes together.

a Sweet Legacy

Glazed Almonds

1 c. whole almonds

1/2 c. sugar

2 T. butter

1/2 t. vanilla

Combine almonds, sugar, and butter in iron skillet, and cook over medium heat. Stir constantly. Sugar will melt and form golden-brown glaze on almonds in approximately 15 minutes. Remove from heat. Stir in the vanilla and spread into small clusters on nonstick foil to cool.

SHELLEY RIPPY

Crunchy Glazed Walnuts

Walnuts are, without question, my husband's "hands down" favorite nut. His favorite ice-cream is black walnut, and his favorite candy is whichever kind is full of walnuts. In fact, one year, my grandmother gave him 2 gallon bags of shelled black walnuts for his birthday! He wrote his name on them and put them in our freezer. If I wanted to make something with walnuts, I had to go buy them because those were spoken for!

a Sweet Legacy

Crunchy Glazed Walnuts

1 c. whole walnut halves

1 c. water

1/4 c. sugar

1/4 c. light corn syrup

2 1/2 T. butter

Place a single layer of walnuts in a shallow pan. Cover with water, and bring to boiling. Boil for 30 seconds; then remove from heat and drain off water.

Pour corn syrup and sugar over walnuts. Stir well and return to heat. Bring mixture to a boil; then reduce heat and simmer for 10 minutes, stirring occasionally to prevent burning.

While mixture is simmering, melt the butter in a nonstick skillet. Using a slotted spoon, remove walnuts from the sugar, and add them to the pan of melted butter, leaving most of the candy sauce behind.

Cook the walnuts in butter, stirring constantly, over medium heat for about 5 minutes or until nuts are brown and crunchy. Use a slotted spoon to lift nuts onto a buttered plate to cool.

Store in an airtight container.

These candied nuts are great for snacking, but they are also the perfect addition to many salads. My mom likes them best added to a salad with goat cheese and pears.

a Sweet Legacy

Honey Almond Nougat

I was born in Port Elizabeth, South Africa, where my parents were missionaries in the late 1960s and early 1970s. This candy is very similar to a nougat candy that is popular there—and one bite takes me right back to my childhood!

This candy is sweet but not too sweet! Perfect for when you just want a "little something." Wrapping the candy in a combination of foil wrappers and clear wrappers makes for a beautiful presentation.

a Sweet Legacy

Honey Almond Nougat

3/4 c. sugar

1 T. corn starch

3/4 c. light corn syrup

1/2 c. honey

1/2 c. water

2 egg whites, beaten

1 c. roasted almonds, see recipe below

2 sheets edible paper

Line bottom and the sides of an 8-inch square foil pan with edible paper. Use small dabs of butter to keep paper in place.

In a large saucepan, combine sugar and cornstarch. Add corn syrup, honey, and water. Cook and stir until sugar dissolves. Stirring occasionally, continue cooking to soft crack stage (286° F).

While syrup is cooking, beat egg whites to stiff peaks. Slowly pour syrup over beaten egg whites while beating constantly with a mixer on high speed. Continue beating until the nougat mixture becomes stiff. Fold in the roasted almonds and pour into prepared pan.

Spread nougat evenly in pan and top with edible paper. Chill until firm. Remove from foil pan and cut into pieces with a buttered knife, and smear a glaze of soft butter on cut edges. Wrap pieces in waxed paper or in wax lined foil wrappers and twist paper ends.

Roasted Almonds

1 c. whole almonds

1/2 t. butter

Roast in cake pan at 350° F for 15 minutes. Stir to coat all almonds with the butter.

a Sweet Legacy

Mexican Orange Candy

My great-grandmother, Jessee, got this recipe while living in West Texas in the early 1900s. So this recipe has been around for a long time! Mexican orange candy is sweet and gooey, and the kitchen smells wonderful because of the fresh fragrant orange rind that is central to this recipe.

a Sweet Legacy

Mexican Orange Candy

1 c. granulated sugar, caramelized

1/4 c. boiling water

2 c. brown sugar

Pinch of salt

The grated rind of 1 or 2 fresh oranges (or 2 T. granulated orange rind)

1 c. chopped nuts (pecans or walnuts)

1 c. evaporated milk or heavy cream

SHELLEY RIPPY

Caramelize the 1 cup of sugar by stirring slowly in a hot frying pan. Shake pan or stir vigorously to prevent burning. Add boiling water to caramelized sugar and boil, stirring constantly until sugar is dissolved. Add remaining 2 cups of brown sugar, cream, and salt. Any remaining hard pieces will begin to melt out. Boil, stirring constantly, until candy reaches 236° F, soft ball stage. Add orange rind, and remove from heat. Beat candy, allowing it to cool a bit before beating in nuts. Pour into a buttered loaf pan, and allow candy to cool. Cut into 1-inch pieces with a sharp buttered knife and wrap in wax lined foil candy wrappers. Alternatively, you can drop by teaspoonful onto waxed paper and wrap in foil candy wrappers.

a Sweet Legacy

Molded Chocolates with Tart Lemon Filling

My son calls these lemon bombs. I believe that is a compliment! The liquid center is a delightful surprise. I like to give close friends an assortment of these lemon creams and cordial cherries for Valentine's Day.

However, these are delicious, unique, and elegant candies for any occasion. They have a gooey liquid center. The creamy lemon filling pairs best with dark chocolate.

a Sweet Legacy

Molded Chocolates with Tart Lemon Filling

2 c. granulated sugar

1/2 c. lemon juice

2 T. light corn syrup

Freshly grated lemon zest from 1 medium lemon, optional

1 lb. dipping chocolate

SHELLEY RIPPY

Chocolate molds, available at any craft store and many grocers.
Small plastic paintbrush to paint the chocolate into the molds.

Lemon Filling:

Prepare your workstation by setting a large baking sheet on a sturdy counter or tabletop and sprinkling it lightly with 2 tablespoons of water or lemon juice.

Combine the sugar, lemon juice, and corn syrup in a medium saucepan over medium heat. Stir until the sugar dissolves; then cover the pan and allow the sugar syrup to boil for 2 minutes to prevent any crystallization on the sides of the pan.

Remove the lid and continue to cook the syrup, without stirring, until it reaches 239° F. Pour the sugar syrup onto the prepared baking sheet. Allow it to sit at room temperature for several minutes. After 2 to 3 minutes, it is ready to be worked.

Dampen a spatula or dough scraper with water, and use the scraper to push the syrup into a pile in the middle of the sheet.

Using a dampened spatula or wooden spoon, begin to "cream," or work, the candy in a figure-eight pattern. Continually scrape the candy into the center, draw a figure eight, and then scrape it together again. At first the candy will be very clear and fluid, but it will gradually become more opaque and creamy. After 5 to 6 minutes, the candy will become stiff—but still very gooey—and harder to manipulate.

At this point, your candy is ready to use. Add the lemon zest, if desired, and transfer candy into a bowl. Cover with plastic wrap and chill while you prepare the chocolate molds.

a Sweet Legacy

Chocolate Molds

Melt 1/2 pound dipping chocolate in a microwave-safe bowl for 30 seconds. Stir to continue melting chocolate. Heat another 15 seconds and stir until smooth. Spoon about 1/2 teaspoon of chocolate into each mold. Use a paintbrush to lift chocolate up onto the sides and into the crevices of the mold you have chosen. Lift mold to light and look up at the underside to determine if molds are fully covered or if you need more chocolate. You want to make sure molds are fully covered so lemon filling won't leak out later.

Allow the chocolate molds to cool and set for about 10 minutes, either on the counter or in the refrigerator. Once chocolate molds are set, they are ready for filling. Spoon about 1/2 teaspoon of lemon cream into each mold. The filling is sticky and gooey, so I find that it is best to use two spoons and drag the filling off the end of one spoon, using the other. The filling will settle and self level in the molds. Chill.

Heat the remaining 1/2 pound of dipping chocolate per the directions above. Use a spoon to drop a little chocolate over each of the molds. Use either the back of a spoon or the paintbrush to smooth and seal each mold, making sure to completely cover the lemon cream to the edges of the mold so it won't leak out of the cooled candy.

Chill in refrigerator until set for about 30 minutes. Turn candy molds onto clean counter or cookie sheet. Gently tap tops of molds or bend plastic mold slightly to loosen candies. They will drop out of the molds. Check each chocolate after a few minutes to see if you need to seal any leaks.

Store candies in refrigerator in air tight container. Makes about 8 molds of 15 – 16 candies per mold.

Peanut Clusters

The love shows in the packaging. Little gold, silver, or red foil cups dress up rum truffles, peanut clusters, or buckeyes. No one will guess how easy they were to make!

a Sweet Legacy

Peanut Clusters

1 lb. White Almond Bark

12 oz. pkg. Bakers semi-sweet chocolate

24 oz. salted Spanish peanuts

Melt almond bark in a 200º F oven. Stir in melted chocolate chips. Add peanuts. Stir to coat nuts. Drop by teaspoon full into mini muffin or candy cups and allow to cool completely.

Pecan Toffee

When it comes to candy, my aunt Linda has the most willpower of anyone in the family. But here is a recipe that even she cannot resist!

91

a Sweet Legacy

Pecan Toffee

1 c. pecans

3/4 c. brown sugar, packed

1/2 c. butter

1/2 c. milk chocolate chips

Butter a 9-x-9-inch pan. Spread pecans in pan. Heat sugar and butter to boiling, stirring constantly. Boil over medium heat, stirring constantly for 7 minutes. Immediately spread mixture evenly over nuts in pan.

Sprinkle chocolate pieces over hot candy. In about a minute, chocolate will melt and can be easily spread over candy using the back of a spoon or a rubber spatula. While still warm, cut into 1 1/2-inch squares. Chill until firm.

Makes 3 dozen candies.

a Sweet Legacy

Buttery Pecan Pralines

Pralines are a great American candy, especially in the South. We took the kids to Chattanooga, Tennessee, to visit the Civil War battlegrounds and learn some US history. They tried the pralines at every gift shop we came across. What Michael and I remember as a sober look at the war that defined our nation, the children remember only by whether the pecans in the pralines there were whole or chopped!

It was hard to keep them away from these pralines long enough to have a photo taken for this book!

a Sweet Legacy

Buttery Pecan Pralines

2 c. sugar

2 c. white corn syrup

1 lb. butter

2 c. heavy whipping cream

2 t. vanilla

7 c. chopped pecans

SHELLEY RIPPY

Cook sugar and corn syrup over medium-low heat until candy thermometer reaches 250º F, the firm ball stage on a candy thermometer. Remove from heat. Add butter, and stir until melted. Add whipping cream slowly. Return to the heat, stirring constantly. Cook until thermometer reaches 242º F. The candy will form a soft ball when dropped in a bowl of cold water.

Remove from heat. Add vanilla and pecans and mix well. Drop on foil sprayed with Pam. (Or we spray mini muffin tins with Pam and fill about 1/2 inch deep.) When cool, wrap pralines in Saran Wrap. Delicious chewy treats.

I included this recipe because it is so heavy in nuts that it is not quite as "gooey" as the Chewy Praline recipe. This is for those who prefer the slightly drier candy.

Chewy Pecan Pralines

Note from Aunt Paula, January 2006:

"I had a great time in our Holiday Sweat…er…I mean Sweet shop!"

The biggest difference between this recipe and the pecan praline recipe is that the nuts are cooked along with the candy in this recipe. This gives the pralines a toasted flavor.

a Sweet Legacy

Chewy Pecan Pralines

1 c. sugar

1 c. light corn syrup

Pinch of salt

1/4 c. butter

7/8 c. evaporated milk

1/2 tsp. vanilla

2 c. pecans

SHELLEY RIPPY

Cook sugar, syrup, and a few grains of salt rapidly to a firm ball stage (242° F), stirring occasionally. The temperature will shoot up very fast once this stage is reached, so be careful not to overheat the syrup or your finished candy may be too hard.

Add butter, milk, and nuts gradually so that mixture does not stop boiling at any time.

Cook over medium heat to soft ball stage (240° F), stirring constantly because mixture sticks easily at the last. About 25 minutes are required for cooking.

Remove from heat. Stir in the vanilla. Work very fast to get the candy out of the hot pan. This candy will continue to cook and harden until it is placed in the muffin tins. It can easily overcook.

Drop into well-buttered muffin tins, filling the bottom third only, as you do not want the pralines to be too thick.

Cool to room temperature. Makes about 30 pieces

a Sweet Legacy

Popcorn Balls

Something about the fall made us long for homemade popcorn balls. My mom would pop the popcorn, and I must have checked the syrup 20 times, barely able to wait for it to finish so we could make the popcorn balls. I can still taste the buttery treat now!

After having my own children, I learned that you always want to make two batches of popcorn balls. The first batch is guaranteed to disappear the first night!

a Sweet Legacy

Popcorn Balls

3 c. sugar

1 c. water

1/2 c. white vinegar

1 T white corn syrup

6 qts. Popcorn

Butter for hands

SHELLEY RIPPY

Put popcorn in a large buttered bowl or casserole dish.

Combine ingredients in a 2-quart saucepan over medium heat. Cook without stirring until candy hardens when dropped in a bowl of water, approximately 295º F on a candy thermometer. Pour hot candy over popcorn and stir with a buttered spatula, and then use generously buttered fingers to shape into balls.

This is extremely *hot*! Generously butter your hands to protect your skin from the hot candy and work very fast to form balls. You can go back and tighten the popcorn balls as they cool. Wrap each one in Saran Wrap.

a Sweet Legacy

Molasses Popcorn Balls

They say variety is the spice of life, so try a little variation on the old popcorn ball recipe and spice up your snack life! The distinctive flavor of molasses is a great addition to this old-fashioned popcorn ball recipe.

Remember, when making any popcorn balls, butter your hands generously and work fast. You want to remember the delicious candy, not burned fingers!

107

a Sweet Legacy

Molasses Popcorn Balls

1 c. molasses

1 c. sugar

1 tbsp. butter

3 qts. popped corn

Put popcorn in a large buttered bowl or casserole dish.

Melt butter in a medium saucepan over medium heat. Add sugar and molasses, and cook to hard crack stage, approximately 295º F on a candy thermometer. A drop of syrup in cold water will be hard and brittle.

Pour hot syrup over popped corn and stir with buttered spoon. Shape into balls with generously buttered hands. You can tighten the balls as they cool. Wrap each popcorn ball in Saran Wrap.

It is important to keep hands well buttered. Syrup will be very hot!

a Sweet Legacy

Pulled Molasses Taffy

Everyone loves pulled taffy! That's why there are so very many taffy flavors to choose from! Taffy is as fun to make as it is delicious to eat. I call it my "therapy" candy because nothing improves a person's disposition quite like pulling taffy!

Let's face it! Taffy ingredients are incredibly sticky! Once you pour out the taffy and it begins to cool, it must be worked continually buy pulling and folding to incorporate enough air into the mix to create the smooth chewy candy texture we love so much. Making taffy requires good humor and a little patience.

Children also love to help pull taffy—enlist their assistance to create a fun family tradition.

Pulled Taffy: So Versatile and Oh, So Delicious!

111

a Sweet Legacy

Pulled Molasses

2 c. molasses

1 c. granulated sugar

3/4 c. water

1/8 t. baking soda

4 T. butter

1/2 t. vanilla

Combine molasses, sugar, and water in a heavy saucepan over medium heat. Boil, stirring occasionally until candy forms a firm ball in cold water, 245 degrees F. Add butter, soda and vanilla and continue cooking, stirring frequently to prevent burning, until candy forms a hard ball when dropped into cold water, 260° F on your candy thermometer.

SHELLEY RIPPY

Remove from heat.

Pour candy onto well-buttered platter. When just cool enough to handle, begin to pull taffy until it lightens in color and becomes porous. It is easiest to work with only half of the taffy at a time. Pull by making a long rope then fold it back on itself and twisting the pieces back together. Repeat the pulling and folding process until taffy stiffens and becomes harder to pull. Form a single twisted rope and cut into 1-inch pieces with buttered scissors. Wrap in waxed paper candy wrappers

a Sweet Legacy

Old-Fashioned Vinegar Taffy

Okay, I admit it! I don't really relish sitting at a table and cutting Saran Wrap into tiny squares and then wrapping up hundreds of tiny pieces of candy. But this is why you have friends! Fortunately, my mother-in-law, Debbie, has the patience to help with this "less fun" task! And the results are more than worth it!

Recently, though, we discovered that wax-coated candy wrappers have become readily available in craft shops like Hobby Lobby or Michael's. They are very inexpensive and come in handy packages of 50 or 100 sheets. They make the job of wrapping a lot more pleasant!

a Sweet Legacy

Old-Fashioned Vinegar Taffy

Vinegar taffy or vinegar candy, as my grandfather used to call it, is a simple and yummy old-fashioned candy that has managed to retain its popularity over time.

2 T. butter

2 c. sugar

1/2 c. vinegar

1/8 t. cream of tartar

1 pinch of salt

Melt butter over medium heat in a heavy saucepan. Add sugar, vinegar, cream of tartar, and salt. Stir until all of the sugar is dissolved. Boil, without stirring, until candy forms a firm ball when dropped in cold water, about 252º F on a candy thermometer. Pour finished candy onto well-buttered dish. Let it rest until it is cool enough to handle. Be careful! Taffy may be cool on the surface but blistering hot beneath!

Once candy is just cool enough to handle, begin to pull taffy until it lightens in color and becomes porous. Pull by making a long rope and then folding it back on itself and twisting the pieces back together. Repeat the pulling and folding process until taffy stiffens and becomes harder to pull. Form a single twisted rope and cut into 1" pieces with buttered scissors. Wrap in waxed paper candy wrappers.

a Sweet Legacy

Rum Truffles

I am featuring rum truffles here because they are my personal favorite. However, this simple recipe can be used to make a variety of truffles. Try substituting bourbon, amaretto, Kaluha, or mint liquor for the rum.

Another great variation is to roll the undipped centers in cocoa powder or finely chopped nuts. Hazelnuts or walnuts work well against the semi-sweet chocolate.

The love shows in the packaging. Little gold, silver, or red foil cups dress up rum truffles, peanut clusters, or buckeyes.

a Sweet Legacy

Rum Truffles

2/3 c heavy whipping cream

3 T. unsalted butter

1 T. sugar

6 squares (6 oz.) semi-sweet baking chocolate, chopped

2 T. rum or other desired liquor

1 c. cornstarch, in a bowl (Omit cornstarch if rolling centers in nuts or cocoa powder)

1 lb. dipping chocolate, chopped

SHELLEY RIPPY

1/4 lb. white, red, or green dipping chocolate (optional). Melt and sling across tops of cooled truffles for a really professional look.

Melt butter, sugar, and semi-sweet chocolate in a cereal bowl in the microwave for 1 minute. Stir until smooth. It may be necessary to heat up to one minute more, stopping to stir every 15 seconds to avoid burning the chocolate. Stir in whipping cream. Continue stirring until all white is combined with the chocolate. Add liquor, and stir until smooth. Cover with plastic wrap, and place in refrigerator for several hours to chill and set. This may be done a day ahead.

Once chocolate is set, slice into 8 sections using a standard table knife. I like working with only one section at a time, as the center chocolate will soften very quickly. Cut or break each section into 4 pieces. With clean and cool hands, gently roll each piece in the palm of your hands to begin to form a ball. Drop onto cookie sheet lined with wax paper.

Once each truffle center has been roughly shaped, place the pan back in the refrigerator for a few minutes to reset so they can be easily handled. Once set, roll each center into a smooth ball by rolling it between the palms of your hands. Roll each center in cornstarch and set on a new sheet of wax paper. Set completed tray back in the refrigerator to harden. The centers are ready to dip.

Follow the instructions on the packaging for how best to heat your chosen dipping chocolate. I prefer Wilton's dark dipping chocolate, which can be heated in a bowl in the microwave. I heat 1/2 the bag at a time.

To dip the chocolate, drop a center into the bowl of dipping chocolate. Then, using a dipping spoon or a long-tined fork, gently lift the chocolate out of the dipping chocolate and inverting the fork, drop it gently onto a sheet of waxed paper. Make a swirling motion as you pull the fork away from the top of the chocolate to create a lovely top.

Once the chocolate is set, I like to embellish the truffles with a little white chocolate. If you choose to do this, melt white chocolate in the microwave for about 30 seconds, and stir out any lumps. Dip the tip of a long-tined fork into the melted chocolate and sling the chocolate across the tops of the finished truffles. Tip: set the truffles on a sheet of wax paper first so all of the mess goes on the paper and not the countertop!

a Sweet Legacy

Turtles

When my family gathers in the fall to make candy, we go through pounds and pounds of nuts and obscene amounts of chocolate. Somehow, we always end up with a bit of dipping chocolate here and there or a partial bag of pecans or walnuts. So it's no surprise that we like to end our weekend by making turtles.

The caramel from the Caramel Nut Roll recipe comes together easily, but watch out! At my house, you may find your turtle has walnuts for his front feet and pecans in the back. Or his shell may be coated in a layer of finely chopped nuts left over from rolling truffles. The fact is, any way you choose to combine caramel, nuts, and chocolate just can't be bad!

Waste not, want not!

For a yummy variation on the traditional turtle, try replacing the nuts with a pretzel. The sweet and salty combination is very good!

a Sweet Legacy

Turtles

24 oz. of whole pecan halves, or walnut halves (about 100 halves)

1 batch of hot caramel from Caramel Nut Roll recipe

16 oz. semi-sweet or milk chocolate chips

1/2 stick paraffin wax

The caramel for this recipe is the same as the caramel in the caramel nut rolls with divinity centers.

SHELLEY RIPPY

On a glass plate or nonstick tray, arrange 3 dozen or so clusters of 4 or 5 pecan halves in a cross or star shape, leaving about 2 inches between each cluster.

Cook caramel exactly as described in the caramel nut roll recipe.

Once caramel is finished, remove from heat and drop by rounded spoonfuls on to the arranged nuts. The weight of the caramel may cause the nuts to shift. Tuck them back under, as required to have 4 "turtle feet" sticking out from under the caramel. Allow to cool completely.

While caramel is cooling, melt chocolate, either over double boiler or in the microwave in a microwave-safe bowl. Chocolate melted in the microwave should be heated in 30 second intervals and stirred in between. When chocolate is nearly melted, add wax. Stir until wax melts completely and chocolate is smooth. If using microwave, you may need to heat chocolate an additional 30 seconds, and then stir the chocolate and paraffin to combine completely.

Spoon melted chocolate over the backs of the turtles. I like to touch the tip of the spoon to the center of the turtle's back and swirl the chocolate as I lift to give a professional look.

a Sweet Legacy

Afterword

My grandmother, Mary, is a wealth of knowledge on any home-economics topic. She is always throwing out a little idiom or fact that helps my recipe be successful. Sayings such as "a pint is a pound the world around," or, "if an egg floats, then you know it's bad."

I asked her once how she managed to remember all of those things, and she said it was the culture she grew up in. She pointed out that my great-grandmother grew up and lived in a completely different culture to my own. In her lifetime, she saw the advent of the car, air travel, space travel, and a landing on the moon. And she was quite grown up before she ever actually rode in a car. What was important, even critical, for her to know and remember was completely different from what we value enough to commit to memory today. She couldn't run out to the store for one missing ingredient or keep her stain remover pen in her purse for spills when not at home. She was poor and somewhat isolated in her West Texas home and had to know and remember how to "make do" with what she had on hand.

My grandmother, too, is a child of a culture more like that of her mother than the culture I grew up in. If I need to remove a stain from the carpet, I just run into my home office and look it up online. If I don't have "it" on hand, I hop in the car and have two stores within a mile of home that probably carry "it." I commit almost nothing to my memory and *everything* to my Palm Pilot organizer or iPhone! So while I am a talented engineer, I live a disposable home life. If "it" has a hole in it, throw it out and buy new. If "it" is too short, sell it on eBay and buy new… On the other hand, Grandma sews, mends, and alters with the same skill at which she quilts, knits, and tats. Growing up, her gifts were exclusively handmade and not store bought.

My grandmother and great-grandmother managed to keep most of these candy recipes in their heads. I rely on my computer, and my children will rely on this book.

127

a Sweet Legacy

SHELLEY RIPPY

Tips and Tricks

Use these tips to help you consistently create beautiful and delicious candies.

Measure precisely! This sounds like a simple thing, but it makes all the difference in candy making and in baking.

It's a good idea to measure ingredients over waxed paper or a garbage bowl rather than over the ingredients already combined for a particular recipe, just in case of spills.

Sugar can be scooped into a measuring cup then the excess scraped off with the back of a table knife. But brown sugar should be firmly packed into the measuring cup and leveled.

Make sure your candy thermometer is reliable. I like the glass tube kind best. My Mom favors the digital kind. I recommend you test your candy thermometer by inserting it in a pot of boiling water. The thermometer should read 212°F. You can adjust your recipe temperature up or down based on your actual measurement. Watch the candy's temperature carefully—higher temperatures create brittle candy and lower temperatures create chewy candy.

Altitude, as well as heat and humidity, can affect candies, such as taffy or caramel—cool, dry days are best for making any candy. You should not make candy on a rainy or very humid day, unless you can remain in a climate-controlled (dehumidified) environment. High humidity causes a sticky surface to form on your candy.

For cutting finished candy, generously grease scissors or a sharp knife with butter to prevent making a sticky mess.

a Sweet Legacy

Store your candy in a dry, airtight container; moisture will make the candy stickier. This is especially problematic with taffy or caramel candies.

Candies such as taffy are very versatile! Try creating your own flavor of taffy by adding fruit or peppermint oil for flavoring. Also, a few drops of food coloring may be added as you pull. But you may want to wear silicone gloves to keep from staining your fingers!

Not all dipping chocolate is the same. It is important to follow the directions on the package to make sure your chocolate melts smoothly. Most dipping chocolate today can be melted in the microwave. Test yours before dragging out your double boiler. Start by heating a small amount in a bowl for 30 seconds. Stir. Heat another 15 seconds then stir again. Continue in that manner for up to a minute, always stopping to stir every few seconds. It is important to keep the chocolate from overheating.

Hot to touch is too hot for dipping. If you get the dipping chocolate too hot, candy centers melt into it or cornstarch from surface of the candy center melts into the chocolate and thickens it. This will cause the dipping chocolate to lose its smooth, silky consistency very quickly.

You can chill or freeze most candy centers, prior to dipping, then use a toothpick to hold the center when you dip it. However, for "fancy" chocolates like rum truffles or chocolate-covered cherries, you will have the most beautiful result using a dipping spoon or a long-tined fork. That allows you to flip the candy onto the plate and swirl the chocolate as you lift away the spoon. The candy has a silky, smooth coating with a sweet little curl on top!

Dipping chocolate that is no longer smooth may still be useful. As long as it is not overcooked, you can use the extra dipping chocolate to top turtles (caramel topped pecan halves) or make peanut clusters. Or you can sling the chocolate over pretzels or fruit…or even hand spoonfuls to the grandchildren.

A dipping spoon is a thin plastic or metal instrument that has the shape of a spoon but is hollow, like a wide loop on the end of a stick. There is very little surface area to come into contact with the candy so you can easily scoop the candy out of the dipping chocolate, flip it onto a plate, and swirl the top as you lift the "spoon" away.

A really lovely way to decorate dipped chocolates is by "slinging" a colored chocolate over the top of the finished candies. Just heat a little bit of white or colored chocolate in a small bowl in the microwave for 30 seconds. Stir to melt. Once the chocolate is smooth and runny, dip the ends of a long-tined fork into the chocolate and literally sling it back and forth or drizzle it across the top of the finished candies. I really enjoy using red and green to accent the candies at Christmas.

My aunt Paula is always reminding me to "sift and save the dust" (finely chopped nut powder) from the chopped nuts when cleaning up after making anything including nuts. We can "recycle" these perfectly good nuts for the caramel nut roll recipe, and the tiny bits are perfect as a coating for truffles.

The key to good fudge is to follow the directions exactly. Use an accurate candy thermometer and make sure you reach the temperatures called for in the recipe before moving to the next step. Undercooked fudge is sugary.

Once you get to soft ball stage, you don't want to stir too much because you can actually promote crystallization of sugar into large grains. If you overbeat the fudge, it will be crumbly and dry. Fudge should be smooth and creamy and melt on your tongue.

Tips for Zesting Lemons: Roll before squeezing. Zest before cutting! Rolling the lemon on the counter before "juicing" ensures you will get the most juice from the lemon. If you need the lemon zest, as in the Tart Lemon Filling recipe, zest the lemon before cutting. It is very difficult to grate a lemon that has been squeezed.

If your recipe calls for brown sugar but you don't have any on hand, check your pantry for molasses. You can substitute a scant cup of sugar and 1 tablespoon of molasses for brown sugar. If the recipe calls for dark brown sugar, use 2 tablespoons of molasses.

Waxed paper can be cut into pieces to wrap the candy, or paraffin-coated, precut candy wrappers are available at stores that carry candy-making supplies, such as Michael's or Hobby Lobby. These are inexpensive and come in handy packages of 50 or 100 sheets.

Yes, you can freeze it! We freeze all of our candies for use or gifting at a later date. Be sure to give candy plenty of time to come up to room temperature before serving. Also, candies like turtles can stick to each other, so arrange frozen turtles on a nonstick platter to thaw. Most candy can last several months in the freezer or up to a month, refrigerated.

Candies that do not have nuts will last longer in the fridge or freezer without becoming sugary than candies with nuts. Keep this in mind if you are making caramel, date candy, or fudge that you want to put away for later.

Packaging the product: Great opportunity to involve younger children.

a Sweet Legacy

Terminology

Almonds "pop" in Almond Toffee recipe: As you heat the raw almonds, they begin to expand, which causes the "popping" sound. This is your cue that the toffee is ready! You have to love a recipe that tells you when it is done!

Caramelize sugar – Recipes like Caramel or Mexican Orange Candy get their warm color and unique toasty flavor from caramelized sugar. To caramelize sugar, simply add plain white granulated sugar to a hot skillet and stir it around. As the sugar reaches 310° F, it will begin to turn brown and liquefy. The longer you cook it, the darker the syrup becomes.

Candy temperature stages: Any decent candy thermometer will list, either on the thermometer itself or on its cover, the candy-making stages defined here. These are a very good guide to help you when a recipe just says "cook to the hard ball stage, or heat until it spins a thread."

However, there are 8 degrees of cooking between soft and firm ball stage, and 25 degrees between hard ball and hard crack! Time and experience has proven that some recipes turn out best if the candy is heated just above or just below the exact temperatures listed here.

That is why in this book I have tried to define both an exact temperature and call out a stage corresponding to the chart below. For instance, in the recipe for cream caramel, I ask you to heat the caramel to 245° F, the firm ball stage. Technically, the candy is just beginning to make a firm ball here. This is the point where the candy holds its shape in cold water and does not emit a powdery residue when you reach in with your fingers to shape it into a ball. If you don't heat the caramel enough, it will never set up

133

a Sweet Legacy

enough to cut and wrap. On the other hand, if you let it get all the way to 248º F, it may be harder than you like. If this happens to you, don't rush to throw it out; soft caramel is great over ice cream, and kids enjoy sucking on hard caramel.

- Spin a thread – Starts at 230º F (110º C) on your candy thermometer
- Soft ball stage – Starts at 240º F (115.5º C) on your candy thermometer
- Firm ball stage – Starts at 248º F (120º C) on your candy thermometer
- Hard ball stage – Starts at 260º F (126.7º C) on your candy thermometer
- Soft crack stage – Starts at 285º F (140.5º C) on your candy thermometer
- Hard crack stage – Starts at 302º F (150º C) on your candy thermometer

Double boiler: A double boiler is simply putting a pan of water on the stove underneath a second pan or bowl of chocolate. The heat from the boiling water is enough to melt the chocolate in the bowl above, without scorching the chocolate. You can buy a double boiler set, but I have always found success with a stainless-steel bowl set on top of a saucepan. However, you do need to be careful. Don't let the water boil dry. Steam escaping from the bottom pan is *hot* and can burn your skin. Also, water droplets in your chocolate will keep it from melting smoothly. For years, a double boiler was required for dipping chocolate. But modern conveniences have erased so much complexity. Most dipping chocolate can be melted in the microwave with excellent results. Refer to the directions on the package, or test a small amount in the microwave before getting out your double boiler.

Edible paper, also called wafer paper, or rice paper, is used in the Honey Almond Nougat recipe and is the only item in this cookbook that may not be readily available at your grocery store. I have always ordered mine over the Internet. It is inexpensive and conveniently arrives at your door; however, you may have to plan a few days in advance of when you want to make the candy.

Paraffin wax is edible and is often added to chocolates to give a glossy finish and help the chocolate remain solid at room temperature. It is widely available in the baking isle of most grocery stores.

SHELLEY RIPPY

Peaks in beaten egg whites: Separate whites from yolks carefully, and do not break the eggs over the bowl of already separated whites. Any yolk in the egg whites will keep the egg whites from becoming fluffy and tall. Egg whites will become frothy as air is whipped into them. After a few minutes, they will become stark white and form lumps then tall stiff peaks that hold their shape when you stop beating. Fluffy egg whites add volume and lightness to many candy recipes.

Rolling boil: Not all boils are the same. A rolling boil is a very fast boil that does not slow or stop when stirred, also called a full boil.

Spin a thread: 230° F on your candy thermometer. Some recipes, such as Divinity, say to heat until the candy spins a thread. As candy syrup cooks, you will notice a thread that appears between the stir spoon and the candy in the pan. At first, this thread is short and fat and breaks easily when you take out the spoon. But as the temperature of the candy reaches about 230° F, the thread will become very long and wispy.

SME, Subject Matter Expert: the official title our family uses to address the expert candy maker for a particular recipe.

a Sweet Legacy

Cooking
Measurement Equivalents

Cooking Weights and Measures

- 1 t = 5 ml
- 1 T = 1/16 cup = 3 t = 15 ml
- 2 T = 1/8 cup = 1 fl oz = 30 ml
- 4 T = 1/4 cup = 2 fl oz = 60 ml
- 8 T = 1/2 cup = 4 fl oz = 120 ml
- 12 T = 3/4 cup = 6 fl oz = 180 ml
- 16 T = 1 cup = 8 fl oz = 240 ml
- 2 cups = 1 pint = 16 fl oz = 480 ml
- 2 pints = 1 quart = 4 c = 32 oz = 960 ml
- 256 T = 1 gallon = 4 qts = 16 c = 128 fl oz = 3.84 l

Temperature Conversion Formulae

- $C = (F-32) * 5 / 9, \quad F = (C * 9 / 5) + 32$
- See "candy temperature stages" under Terminology for Celsius temperatures defined by cooking stage.

a Sweet Legacy

Endnotes

Family gatherings to craft, sew, or make candy may seem insignificant. It is only after you view them through the wisdom of many years that you realize they were really some of the most significant and important experiences of your life.

When my great-grandmother began collecting these recipes while working in a small confectionary in Kansas, she didn't give a thought to how they would be passed down and cherished by her children and theirs. She was just trying to earn a living.

But by sharing these recipes with her daughters and her daughter's daughters, she began a sweet legacy that is still enriching our family today. The simple act of gathering to spend a few days making candy together each year is part of the glue that binds my family together.

Fortunately, you do not have to have a hundred years of family candy making behind you to create the sweets described in the pages of this book. We are honored to share our sweet legacy with your family. So grab the sugar and some close friends, and start cooking!

This is a legacy that was gifted to me that I am already passing on to my own three children. Remember, it is never too early, or too late, to start a new family tradition.

a Sweet Legacy